Loose Ends

Eldonna Bouton

LOOSE ENDS

A Journaling Tool for Tying up
The Incomplete Details of Your Life and Heart

Eldonna Bouton

Whole Heart Publications
P.O. Box 14358
San Luis Obispo, CA
93406-4358

ATTENTION ORGANIZATIONS, HEALING CENTERS AND SCHOOLS OF SPIRITUAL DEVELOPMENT: Quantity discounts are available on bulk purchases of this book for educational purposes or fundraising. For information contact Whole Heart Publications at the address below.

Published by Whole Heart Publications
P.O. Box 14358
San Luis Obispo, CA
93406-4358

Phone: 805-543-8640
e-mail:info@whole-heart.com
http://www.whole-heart.com

Front cover illustration by Shirley Goetz
Printed by McNaughton-Gunn
Cover design by Keith Bergher & Holly Leighton
Back cover photograph by William Bouton

Manufactured in the USA

ISBN 0-9670384-0-5

See back page for ordering information.

DEDICATION

This book is dedicated to Jacob, my son,
and Bill, my moon

...and to you, courageous reader and writer of heart.

In Memory of Mom,

who stuck around long enough to finish.

ACKNOWLEDGEMENTS

The author would like to thank the following people for their contributions and support in the writing of this book:

Bob Banner for allowing me to pick the left side of his brain, Catherine Haynes for the Pagemaker Vulcan Mind Meld, Shirley Goetz who took a vague notion and created a beautiful illustration, my writing buddies at LWW, Ingrid Reti and Reti's Riters for rooting me on, Marcia Alter, Laura Bedford, Kathryn DeVries, and Valerie Mott who love and believe in me, Keith Bergher and Holly Leighton for their design expertise, Dave Fleming at McNaughton-Gunn, Wayne Miller who taught me that html is not as bad as a root canal, all my clients who keep showing up, John McFadden who seems to think my friendship is worth listening to all my fears and self-doubts, and Clay McPherson my loyal writing partner and number one fan club.

And to my very patient husband and son who held my hands and wiped my brow as I gave birth to this book.

CONTENTS

"When you were born, you cried and the world rejoiced.

Live your life so that when you die, the world cries and

you rejoice."

Cherokee Expression

INTRODUCTION

I was walking among the beautiful foothills near Cerro San Luis early one morning when the light was just right. I looked around, full of gratitude for this glorious place where I live and I thought, "If I died today, I'd die a happy woman."

That thought was immediately followed by, *What if I really was to die today? There are so many things I want to do. And so many things that need to be said.*

When my mother got the call from her doctor eight years ago confirming that she indeed had bone cancer and probably had six months to live, the first thing she did was turn to me and say, "I'm so sorry." She didn't need to say why...we both knew...but she *did* need to *say* it. And I needed to hear it.

I spent the rest of my walk through the hills thinking about all the words I've never gotten around to saying. If I found out I only had six months to live, what would I want to say and how would I say it?

I know I'd want to communicate to each of my children how special they are. I'd want to tell my granddaughter, whom I've only seen once, that distance has not kept me from loving her. I'd want a very special high school teacher to know how much she impacted me. I'd want my ex-husband to know that in spite of our differences, I will cherish some very good times we had together. And the list goes on and on.

This book was born of that beautiful morning walk. I'll bet that you, like me, are probably carrying around a lot of unspoken words to those you love or have loved, those you may have hurt, and those who have hurt you. Think about all the misunderstandings never defended, secrets kept, and hurts unhealed that you've held onto.

What if you were told you only had six months to live? How much shame, remorse or guilt have you lugged around for lo these many years? What would you like to get off your chest?

This book is a tool for you to tidy up all those loose ends. You need not be old or terminally ill to benefit from the exercises contained in this book. On the contrary, this book is designed to help you let go of the past so that you *can* live.

As a massage therapist I regularly see people hoping to release their imbedded emotional baggage. Week after week they climb onto my table for physical and spiritual healing, yet week after week they return with the same stuff they pledged be free of in their last session. Sometimes I get the feeling they scoop up all they meant to leave behind on the way out the door and stuff it back into that pack they've become so accustomed to carrying around on their shoulders. Oh, the comfort of misery's familiarity.

Here's your chance to have your say and leave your bag at the door for good. Be honest. Nobody but you will ever see your words unless you choose to share them. There is benefit in the process of speaking your heart, whether or not you share your truths with another.

There are no rules. You can scribble, tear, swear or cry on these pages. It's your book.

You can start anywhere in the book you like. You don't have to do every exercise (some may not apply to you). You can skip any pages you don't like. You can make copies of and mail any of the letters you've written, tear them up, or leave some or all of them in the book. In fact, when you're finished you will have the opportunity to burn the book if you're the kind of person for whom ritual helps to imbed the process. Remember, there are extra pages in the back of the book if you need them. Some of us have a lot to say. Or, like me, have a large family. Or you can use a blank journal to do the exercises.

A few suggestions:

1. Wait until you have quiet, uninterrupted space to do the exercises.

2. Buy a great pen, one that feels good in your hand.

3. Don't judge yourself as you write. Write as if no one will ever see what you're writing. The point is about saying what's on your mind and in your heart, not about pleasing someone else. So kick the parent, the critic and the editor out of the room.

4. Call it good. When you're finished, don't pore over all the letters and lists. The idea is to be *done* so you can move on.

5. Breathe.

A FEW WORDS ABOUT FORGIVENESS

A friend of mine said she'd read somewhere that the original Sanskrit meaning of forgiveness is "to untie." I've not been able to confirm this, but I like it and since it fits in so well with the title of this book, I'm mentioning it here.

People often ask me, "How can I possibly forgive my (rapist, abuser, ex-wife etc.)? Are you saying I should let them off the hook after what they did to me?"

When I hear these words, I offer the following advice: It is *you* that are being let off the hook. Imagine the person you cannot forgive as someone who once held a fishing pole. They've set down the pole and gone on to other things, perhaps even hurting others. In the meantime, you are still floundering in the murky waters of the past, snagged on their hook. As long as you are spending precious energy resenting, hating and being angry, you will be unable to swim freely. What I am asking you to do is to gently remove the hook that keeps you entangled in the past.

Think of forgiveness as letting go of being responsible for the other person's accountability. I realize that this means releasing the control you may feel this gives you over the person or situation, however, it is *you* that is truly being controlled by the refusal to let go.

A very wise friend of mine whom I've never met, since she is a light that twinkles on the other end of the Internet somewhere, put it like this: Think of your abuser as a horse who is stepping on your foot. You stand there screaming in pain and ranting at the horse. Why not lift the horse's leg up and take it off your foot? In that way your foot can begin to heal and you can let the horse move away from you.

Forgiveness is not an easy thing for a lot of us. I believe that this is because we associate forgiveness with allowing another to "get away with" whatever it is that he or she has done. If someone has done you harm, they will be accountable for their actions with or without your anguish. However seen in a new light, forgiveness can be a way of setting yourself free.

"Dream as if you'll live forever.
Live as if you'll die today."

James Dean

MOTHERS

"What is it about the relationship of a mother that can heal or hurt us? Her womb is the first landscape we inhabit. It is here we learn to respond- to move, to listen, to be nourished and grow."

Terry Tempest Williams, *Refuge*

Write a letter to your mother. Tell her all the things you love about her. Tell her anything you've always wanted to tell her.

Maybe there's a lot of stuff in the letter about how she messed up. Fine. Now forgive and move on.

(If you were raised by someone other than your birth parents, write a letter to that person. There's a separate exercises for adoptees.)

FATHERS

"It doesn't matter who my father was, it matters who
I remember he was."

Anne Sexton

Now, write a letter to your father. Again, say what you need to say. Don't hold back.

UNKNOWN PARENTS

"Not flesh of my flesh/Nor bone of my bone/But miraculously my own. /Never forget for a single minute/ You didn't grow under my heart, /But in it."

Anonymous

If you were adopted or never knew your biological parents, write a letter telling them everything you'd like them to know about you. Tell them what they have missed and what you've always wondred. If you have questions for them, ask.

CHILDREN

"We find delight in the beauty and happiness of children that makes the heart too big for the body."

Ralph Waldo Emerson, *The Conduct of Life*

Write a letter to each of your children. Tell them about their births. Relate your favorite memories of them. Tell each child what makes them special or unique.

_____

_____

_____

_____

_____

_____

_____

_____

_____

_____

_____

_____

_____

_____

_____

PARTNERS

"And when I consider my marriage, no matter where I am, I enter a different place, a kind of shelter, a white room."

Richard Louv, *The Web of Life*

Write a letter to your partner or spouse. Tell him or her why you chose them. Tell them everything you wish they knew about the way you feel.

EXES

"I still miss those I loved who are no longer with me but I find I am grateful for having loved them..."

Rita Mae Brown

If you are separated or divorced, write a letter to your ex. Remember what attracted you to him or her in the first place. Remember why you left. Say what you've always wished you could say.

You can.

THE UNBORN

"And then it dawned on me–I was losing not my life but
my soul. In the rush of my blood and the stream of my
tears, I could feel it leaving my body...the sacrifice of
this tiny seed of a child that had awakened the mother
in me."

Gabrielle Roth, *Sweat Your Prayers*

Write a letter to your child, whether miscarried, stillborn, or aborted. What would you like to tell the child who never made it from your womb to your arms?

This exercise is for men, too. You may not have a womb, but you can still grieve the loss or write as a partner in the experience.

_____

_____

_____

_____

_____

_____

_____

_____

_____

_____

_____

_____

_____

_____

_____

SIBLINGS

"If you cannot get rid of the family skeleton, you may as well make it dance."

George Bernard Shaw

Write a letter to each of your siblings. Tell them how it was to be their sister or brother. What did you learn from them?

If there is anyone on this list who had a negative impact on your life, let `er rip. Then forgive and move on.

SPECIAL RELATIONS

"The most important single influence in the life of a person is another person...who is worthy of emulation."

Paul D. Shafer

Write a letter to a favorite relative. It might be a grandparent or a special aunt or uncle. Tell them why they are important to you and how your life is richer for having known them.

FAVORITE TEACHERS

"The greatest and simplest power of a teacher is the environment of their own freedom and joy."

Jack Kornfield, *A Path with Heart*

Write a letter to a favorite teacher(s) who had a positive influence on you. If he or she is still living, send it. You'll make their day.

I promise.

UNFAVORITE TEACHERS

"Keep away from people who try to belittle your ambitions. Small people always do that, but the really great make you feel that you, too, can become great."

Mark Twain

Write a letter to a terrible teacher. Tell them how wrong they were about you.

Then forgive and move on.

BEST FRIENDS

"Give me one friend, just one, who meets the needs
of all my varying moods."

Esther M. Clark

Write a letter to your best friend. Maybe you have more than one.

Tell your best friend how much he or she means to you. How grateful you are for the shoulder provided, the sniveling listened to, the laughs shared. Relate your favorite memories. Tell your best friend why he or she is just that.

That's what friends are for.

_____

_____

_____

_____

_____

_____

_____

_____

_____

_____

_____

_____

_____

_____

_____

_____

THE BOSS

"If you don't ask, you don't get."

Mahatma Gandhi

Write a letter to your boss. Is there anything you're holding inside that would make for a better relationship if it were out in the open?

Is there anything you'd like to say that you can't say to his or her face without losing your job?

Then go ahead and write it just because you'll feel better. Won't you?

THE CHILD WITHIN

"Children robbed of love, will dwell on magic."
Barbara Kingsolver, *Animal Dreams*

Get a mental picture of your five-year-old self. What would you tell him or her?

Write a letter to that child. Offer lots of comfort and praise. Offer your lap.

MISUNDERSTANDINGS

"Know all, and you will pardon all."

Thomas a' Kempis

Write about a time when you were misunderstood. Tell your side of it.

There. Doesn't that feel better?

OLD WOUNDS

"Let go of your rage. Let go of your anger. Forgive.
Pay attention. Let your own inherent gentleness free
you.

Geri Larkin, *Stumbling Toward Enlightenment*

Write a letter to someone who hurt you.

I've taken into consideration that you might need extra pages in the back for this one. (You may have a list.)

Go ahead and get mad. Let them know how you felt.

Then forgive and move on.

_____

_____

_____

_____

_____

_____

_____

_____

_____

_____

_____

_____

_____

_____

GUILT

"From the body of one guilty deed a thousand ghostly fears and haunting thoughts proceed."

William Wordsworth

Write a letter to someone you may have hurt. Explain why you did what you did at the time. Tell them how sorry you are.

Now, forgive yourself and move on.

MORE FROM THE CHILD

"Seek the wisdom of the ages, but look at the world through the eyes of a child."

Ron Wild

Get that five year old back here. Now, let him or her write a letter to you.

What would he or she tell you?

SHOULD'S

"The only way to get rid of responsibilities is to discharge them."

Walter S. Robertson

Make a list of all the things you think you "should" do in this lifetime. You know, read the classics, learn sign language for the deaf, reframe all your photos.

Now, cross everything off the list you really don't want to do.

You have just been excused.

REGRETS

"To regret deeply is to live afresh"

Thoreau, Journal, November 13, 1839

Write about what you regret. Go ahead, get it over with. Be kind to yourself.

SECRETS

"Forgive our hidden past, the secret shames, as we consistently forgive what others hide."

Jesus, *Prayers of the Cosmos*

Tell a secret you've kept, either by force or by choice. Let it out. You don't have to keep it any more.

Keep breathing.

PETS

"Animals are such agreeable friends-they ask no questions, they pass no criticisms."

George Eliot, "Mr. Gilfil's Story",

Write a letter to each of your pets, living or dead. Really. Don't you wish they knew how you feel about them?

Thank them for being in your life.

LOST LOVED ONES

"How do we grieve? Awkwardly. Imperfectly. Usually with a great deal of resistance. Often with anger and attempts to negotiate. Ultimately by surrendering to the pain."

Melody Beattie, *The Language of Letting Go*

Write a letter to someone who has died that you never got a chance to tell how you felt about him or her.

YOUR BODY

"Here in this body are the sacred rivers: here are the sun and moon, as well as all the pilgrimage places. I have not encountered another temple as blissful as my own body."

Saraha

Write a letter to your body. Thank each wonderful part for supporting your existence. Be nice. Especially to the parts you may think have let you down.

YOUR WISE SELF

"If I had my life to live over, I would start barefoot earlier in the spring and stay that way later in the fall. I would go to more dances. I would ride more merry-go-rounds. I would pick more daisies."

Nadine Stair, If I Had My Life to Live Over

Get a mental picture of your ninety-year-old self. What wisdom would you like him or her to share?

Ask.

SELF-FORGIVENESS

"Her breasts and arms ached with the beauty of her own forgiveness."

Meridel LeSueur

Write a letter to yourself in which you forgive yourself for every time you messed up, missed out, took the wrong turn, said the wrong thing.

Mean it.

GRATITUDE

"i thank You God for most this amazing day; for the leaping greenly spirits of trees and a blue true dream of sky; and for everything which is natural which is infinite which is yes."

ee cummings

Fill the following pages with everything you are grateful for. Add more.

Keep going.

_____

_____

_____

_____

_____

_____

_____

_____

_____

_____

_____

_____

_____

_____

_____

_____

YOUR EPITAPH

"And at the end of your days, you will bless your life because you have done what you came here to do."

Dr. Elisabeth Kubler-Ross, *The Wheel of Life*

Write your own epitaph. What would you put on your tombstone? For what do you want people to remember you?

Give this page to someone you trust to read at your funeral.

Or not.

YOUR FUNERAL

"Dying doesn't cause suffering. Resistance to dying does."

Terry Tempest Williams, Refuge

Speaking of funerals, do you want to be cremated or buried? Would you like to donate your organs? Do you want flowers? What kind?

What music would you like at your service? Do you even want a service? Is there someone that only you know that you want to be notified of your death? Make your wishes known.

It's your funeral after all.

_____

_____

_____

_____

_____

_____

_____

_____

_____

_____

_____

_____

_____

_____

GOD

"And after a long, lonesome and scary time…the people listened and began to hear…And to see God in one another…and in the beauty of the Earth. And Old Turtle smiled. And so did God."

Old Turtle, by Douglas Wood and Cheng-Khee Chee

Write a letter to God. It doesn't matter whether you are Christian or Buddhist or Agnostic. Your God might be Earth or the Great Spirit or the Divine within yourself.

Let your heart speak. Be thankful. Be curious. Be awed.

Wonder on the page.

MORE LOOSE ENDS

"There are only two ways to live your life. One is as though nothing is a miracle. The other is as if everything is."

Albert Einstein

Do you have any other loose ends? Use any remaining pages to tie them up. Perhaps you'd like to write about how you'd do things differently. Or maybe you want to make a list of things you really do want to do before you die.

(Then do them.)

TYING IT ALL UP

"What I have found is. Anything one keeps hidden should now and then be hidden somewhere else."

Elizabeth Bowen, *The Death of the Heart*

Now, make copies of the letters you want to send.

You have two choices. You can keep the book to add to (or in case you need reminding what you've let go of) or you can get rid of it. If you decide to keep it, be sure you have a great hiding place if you don't want anyone else to read it.

If you feel like you've completed the exercises and now you want to be "done", you may choose to throw this book away. Or, if you like, you can have a burning ceremony as a ritual for letting go of the past. Just remember that it is about letting go of what was, so you can be with what is.

You are what is...

_____

_____

_____

_____

_____

_____

_____

_____

_____

_____

_____

_____

_____

_____

_____

_____

_____

_____

_____

_____

_____

_____

_____

_____

_____

_____

_____

_____

_____

_____

_____

_____

_____

_____

_____

_____

_____

_____

_____

_____

_____

_____

_____

_____

_____

_____

_____

_____

_____

_____

_____

_____

_____

_____

_____

_____

_____

_____

_____

_____

_____

_____

_____

_____

_____

_____

_____

_____

_____

_____

_____

_____

_____

_____

_____

_____

_____

_____

_____

_____

_____

_____

_____

_____

_____

_____

_____

_____

_____

_____

_____

_____

_____

_____

ABOUT THE AUTHOR

Eldonna Bouton is a nationally certified massage therapist and owner/practitioner of A KNEADED TOUCH in San Luis Obispo, CA. She has published inspirational nonfiction as well as essays, humor and fiction. She is currently working on a novel and a collection of massage stories to be published in 2000.

A self-proclaimed closet dancer, she has facilitated Spontaneous Dance workshops as a form of inner expression through movement. She is also a therapeutic massage instructor.

Eldonna Bouton currently offers "Loose Ends" workshops on the Central California Coast where she lives with her husband Bill, son Jaob, and loyal canine companion Slim.

We'd love to hear from you...

The Author would like to hear from readers who have benefited from the exercises in "Loose Ends". We would also like feedback on how we might improve our next edition of this book. Did any of the exercises trigger an "I wish there was a page for...?"

Would you like to contribute to our next book?

We're working on a collection of letters from readers who are willing to share any of the letters they have written based upon the exercises in "Loose Ends". All letters will be printed anonymously and any names within the letter will be changed, however we do need your name and address for permission to publish.

Send your correspondence to Whole Heart Publications, P.O. Box 14358, San Luis Obispo, CA, 93406-4358 or contact us via the Internet:info@whole-heart.com or http://www.whole-heart.com

We look forward to hearing from you!

TO ORDER MORE BOOKS

By Phone: Call Whole Heart Publications directly at 805-543-8640.

Via The Internet: Books can also be ordered using Visa or MasterCard on the Internet at http://www.whole-heart.com

By Mail: Send check or money order for $13.95 plus $3.00 shipping for each book to: Whole Heart Publications, P.O. Box 14358, San Luis Obispo, CA, 93406-4358. California residents add $1.01 (7.25%) sales tax to total.